ARMS

SPRAWL

Included

S. E. McKenzie

S. E. MCKENZIE

ARMS: Sprawl included

DEDICATION
To everyone who has been left out in the cold.

S. E. MCKENZIE

This book is a book of speculative fiction. Characters, companies, governments, places, events, are either products of the author's imagination or used fictitiously. Any resemblance to persons (living or dead), companies, governments, places and/or events, is a coincidence.

ARMS: Sprawl included

TABLE OF CONTENTS

S. E. MCKENZIE

ARMS

ARMS: Sprawl included

ARMS

I

Hold me
You, across the sea
Hold me so I can feel

Security

In this land too expensive to be free
We need a lot more money
We need a lot more harmony

Not through guns and steel

But from arms
That will help us heal.
You know what I mean

And you know what I have seen
The world is full of so much heavy stuff
But none of it can replace love.

We don't need to flee
For we have already found
A land which gives us immunity

S. E. MCKENZIE

And time to beat the skin drum

In the downtown core
Prison city
No appeal to the human good

Easier to delete
With free needles
But no free lunch to eat

Buildings in this ghetto part of town
Were torn down
While status would always reflect what you could get

Behind this rampart
Of stone
You never felt so alone

As you climb the hill
Did you feel the elevation?
Or was it all in the mind

ARMS: Sprawl included

To be cruel or to be kind
To see or be
Willfully blind

So much need for power
Whenever there is fear
And there will never be a wall

High enough
To keep all the fear
Out of Bobby's heart

"The wall
Will just tear us apart,"
Anna Marie said

Before they went to bed
"The world is already so torn
What will it be like when he is born?"

S. E. MCKENZIE

"Innocent
And helpless
And in your arms

He will thrive
And love to be alive
He will grow and he will survive,"

Bobby replied
Hoping he had not lied
While Anna Marie cried.

And the rampart had to end
As the river's torrents began to bend
We needed a new guard

For the wall was not high enough
To protect us from this world
So cold, without love

Until the world
Was willing to trade
Arms of war

ARMS: Sprawl included

For plowshares
To end all this hunger
Which was surrounding these banks

Of gold and cold water.
Hold me,
You, across the sea

For we need
Our arms to be linked
So we can feel tranquility

II

The prison city was divided
No one wanted it that way
So Bobby and Anne Marie

Bought a chalet on the hill
The view gave them such a thrill
And no one knew and no one saw

How the fire began
The fire engine sat on the road
And was told that they were in

The wrong jurisdiction

S. E. MCKENZIE

And were not allowed to do a thing
So the authorities stood on the hill
And took a video

Of the fire burning to share the thrill

The video was seen by all
And everyone knew what they could not do
For that was the way of the prison city

How could this be
That they did not do a thing
Everyone was in charge

But no one had responsibility
They were just doing their job
And doing what they were told

As the fire burned their home down
Anne Marie cried
And Bobby's hope died

ARMS: Sprawl included

How could this be
Bobby asked everyday
How could we lose everything

So quickly that day
No one replied
For they were living in a prison city

III
Tom and Joe had a dream
That they wanted to actualize
So they rented a shop in the lower part of town

And put up as sign
The traffic flow was wild and free
For it was connected to the open economy

To their dismay
One day
A no entry sign was put in the way

Tom and Joe
Sat and watched
As the new store that sold the same thing

S. E. MCKENZIE

Opened down the street
Private drive
Made it right

The city officials said
A public drive was too much risk
Better for the traffic to drive by

As their debt piled up
The nightmare grew
Tom and Joe were no longer welcome anywhere

The traffic flow was redirected
And Tom and Joe
Sat and waited

Tom's wife Trish
Had one wish
And that was to avoid being ruined

The rules were slanted
Against the poor
And everyone knew to lock their door

ARMS: Sprawl included

That official oppression
Was just a new rule
And to disobey you would be talked to as a fool

Trish was tired
And the her baby just grew
She walked to the river

And just fell in
And no one knew how or when
Heaven's door had opened the gate

Victorian Culture energy flow
Complacent and so eager to grow
At the speed of light through the internet

Oppressive but so ingrained
The look of sadness and inner pain
Was shared so only a few went insane

The pain was often mistaken
For anger and hate
Even though fear was so obvious and rampant

S. E. MCKENZIE

Controlled so many as paralysis set in
Possibly how Trish fell in
The river so unforgiving

Reflected reality all around
Nothing to work with
No arms to hold

The days of the old
Victorian Victory
Locked away in mystery

The historian had nothing more to say
All we could do was close our eyes and pray
Hoping for a better way

A cloud from the past
Made us doubt ourselves unless authorized
We were criticized

ARMS: Sprawl included

While hidden caverns in the ground
Owned by ghosts from the past
Dead but still could pull

The future into the Abyss

Without saying a word
For ghosts never spoke
And they never awoke

But what they left behind
From days gone by so Victorian
Could dismay

And Trish was with them now everyday
For it took strength to cope
During times of official oppression

Never out of sight
Could be seen
During a starless night.

S. E. MCKENZIE

IV
Hold me
You, across the sea
Hold me so I can feel

Serenity
For my land is haunted
By days gone by

And these ghosts do not sleep in the sky
For they rest below my feet
Within hidden caverns

Dug through hard labor during a time gone by

One day these caverns could reopen
And swallow
Whoever may be nearby

Their loved ones would wonder why
And would look for someone to blame
But no one took responsibility

For they were from a time gone by
A long time ago
A time of great sorrow

ARMS: Sprawl included

For many left their land of nativity
To find this place which gives
So many immunity

From the burdens of the past
Burdens from the industry of war
Burdens of servitude

To an authority
No one knew by name
It refused to take responsibility

Hold me
You, across the sea
Hold me so I can feel

Your arms of peace
Around me
Until the end of time

THE END

S. E. MCKENZIE

SPRAWL

SPRAWL

I

Saul's Sprawl
Urban decay
So bad everyone moved away

Not yet ready to let go
Of life
To give to another.

Saul; so trapped in his own subjectivity
He enjoyed his bias of negativity
Made him feel twice the man

He could no longer be
For his life
Was growing shorter

As the days turned
Into a process
Some believed to be

External Infinity

S. E. MCKENZIE

The possibility of another way
Defied the autocracy.
So let the good inside all

Pave the way to institute the Rights of Man

The one way autocracy wanted it all
Refused to share with other segments
Across the demographic range

Fluid and strange.

"We like it this way
For we detest disturbance and static
We like everything very quiet."

Billy Joe shook his head
And went out to check for mail
He was waiting for a letter

From his true love Sally Anne.
For he knew he loved her the most.
The mail box was rusty

Held by wire and tied to a post
Kept the property value down
Prime land on a river bed and so close to the sea

ARMS: Sprawl included

The dictator called this an atrocity
And his frown
Was just the beginning of his ferocity

Ghost Town
Fear of the unknown
Slander and decay

No better way
To destroy
Goodwill

Of an old time city
Crashing down
Wearing a frown

Billy Joe and Sally Anne
Still found love
It was a miracle, many said

For Billy Joe and Sally Anne

S. E. MCKENZIE

Were living in separate worlds.
She promised to write
And he promised not to fight

As the old time city
Was shaped by hierarchy
From years gone by

Fear of the unknown lurking behind every wall
For Speed Traps were everywhere
No sign of what was yet to come

Old Souls from years gone by
Watched
As the ones who stood their ground

Hanged on
Refusing to fall
Back stabbing was replaced with sharing

Dirt and misinformation
Replaced by a kinder systemization
Which oversaw Idle Talk.

ARMS: Sprawl included

How important one feels
While kicking down another
Conflict between little sister and big brother

One way talk
As the Old Souls grow older
Almost dead but holding on to a string

They liquidate what they can
For they can buy anything
Before they die; too old to cry

Wearing a smile they know how to lie
Victim's hands tied behind their back
Easier to win that way they say

Of an old time city
Crashing down
Wearing a frown

Always putting strangers down
Speed trap
Money grab

S. E. MCKENZIE

Old Souls almost dead
So jealous are they
Of your new life

Their rage grows with age
How feeble they feel
Lost in their Idle Talk

The members
Of the Old Souls' Club
Are searching for a new pill

For they are always ill
And want internal youth
Contrary to external truth

Never too old
For a new thrill
They can still smile before they order a new bill

Sometimes the new bill
Will kill silently
Even though the Idle Talk

ARMS: Sprawl included

Grows quite loudly
Always putting you down
Wearing a frown

Puppet show
They think they know
The rules that make others fools

Feel the glory
In domination
So subjective

See those people
Labelled so conveniently
Not to dehumanize intentionally

But to objectify in order to control
Call them a name after their role
So blinded by the power it brings

Feel the glory
It will make you sing
Onto this steely thing

S. E. MCKENZIE

Of this blood sport sensation
Idle Talk
Misinformation

The truth more than opinion.
A fact not yet owned
And often distained and lost in pain

The need to dominate
Creates fate
Hides hate

The truth will be taken to the grave
The gate keeper flowing through the sky
Must filter so the spread of toxicity
Does not get by.

The keeper will see through hypocrisy
Will hold a place for judgment
And a place of rest

A place to see
Through hypocrisy
Spoken in Idle Talk

ARMS: Sprawl included

Deference to the old soul
Without a name
Roams through sprawl raging blame

Autocratic regime
One way power
Could only destroy the dream

"We know all about you,"
The ghostly voice said to Billy Joe.
"We will be watching you."

Sally Anne
Wrote a letter
That her Momma hid away

"We don't want you near a boy like that,"
Sally Anne heard her mother say
"Billy Joe listens to his own drummer;

And that is not the new way;
You must find a man
Who fits the plan

So you can be part of this new autocracy.

S. E. MCKENZIE

For we are better than him
In everyway
And we use science to prolong our stay.

II
Billy Joe felt intimidation
A new sensation
For his lost generation.

Idle talking
Idol walking
Winding up full of hate

Doing it to intimidate.
Obsolete City
Old ways that create

Fear of the unknown
An excuse for hate
Is so out of date

Feel the rage
Not enough to eat
Grows with age

ARMS: Sprawl included

Ancient city
Guarded by feeble minds
From days gone by

In a Land so rich
No one needs to be neighborly
Hate mongering, fear mongering

Transmitted by the speed of light
Put a person on the list
Spread the fear around

Never missed

Lateral violence
Micro aggression
Hysteria by suggestion

Condemned when condemning
Feud grew too intense
For Billy Joe and Sally Anne

S. E. MCKENZIE

To understand
It wasn't about love
It wasn't about land

It was all about following the plan
And maintaining control of power.
Forcing those weaker and meeker to kneel down

To the invisible hand
Never taking a stand
To protect the Rights of Man

III
Rhetoric replaced common sense
Poison replaced hope
Projection of the negative

Right through the wall
Very little space
In all this sprawl.

Social vampire
Sucked
Psychic fuel

ARMS: Sprawl included

Gave the social vampire
An energy surge
And social position

Revival of the inquisition

And the feud continued
As the rival
Exceeded all expectation

Count all your coins
Stack them in a big pile
Take a selfie

And let the memory linger.
Reckless with all his hate
The social vampire

Was never too late
Too collect his cash
To add to his stash

S. E. MCKENZIE

He would save every dime
Forgot life was all about time
Not just about growing an empire

While using force
Slander
And waste

The social vampire's youth
Was soon gone.
Now he was old and bitter

The social vampire
Vowed to never quit,
So he took a new name and hid.

THE END

ARMS: Sprawl included

Produced by S.E. McKenzie Productions
First Print Edition February 2015

S. E. MCKENZIE

Enquiries: 1(778)992-2453
Mailing Address:
S. E. McKenzie Productions
168 B 5th St.
Courtenay, BC
V9N 1J4

Email Address:
messidartha@aol.com

http://www.amazon.com/SarahMcKenzie/e/B00H9RWX
48/ref=ntt_dp_epwbk_0

www.ingramcontent.com/pod-product-compliance
Lightning Source LLC
Chambersburg PA
CBHW060547030426
42337CB00021B/4467